THE OLD FARMER'S ALMANAC
ENGAGEMENT
CALENDAR 2021

Begin the new year square with every man.

–Robert B. Thomas, founder of
The Old Farmer's Almanac (1766–1846)

D1410644

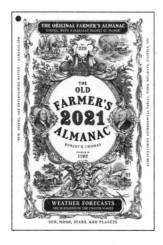

A PLANNER FILLED WITH FUN FACTS, LORE, AND MORE!

Publisher: Sherin Pierce

Editorial: Tim Clark, *writer;* Heidi Stonehill, *editor;* Catherine Boeckmann,
Christopher Burnett, Jack Burnett, Benjamin Kilbride, Sarah Perreault, Janice Stillman

Art director: Colleen Quinnell

Production: David Ziarnowski, *director;* Brian Johnson, *manager;*
Jennifer Freeman, Janet Selle, Susan Shute

Astronomical events are given in Eastern Time.

Cover art: Nongkran_ch/Getty Images

If you find this calendar, please return it to:

Name _____

Address _____

Phone (Home) _____ (Work) _____ (Cell) _____

To order more copies of this calendar, call 800-ALMANAC (800-256-2622)
or visit our Web site at Almanac.com/Shop.
For retail information, contact Stacey Korpi at 800-895-9265, ext. 160.

Printed in China by R. R. Donnelley

ISBN: 978-1-57198-859-1

2021

bold = *U.S. and/or Canadian national holidays*

JANUARY

S	M	T	W	T	F	S
					1	2
3	4	5	6	7	8	9
10	11	12	13	14	15	16
17	**18**	19	20	21	22	23
24	25	26	27	28	29	30
31						

FEBRUARY

S	M	T	W	T	F	S
	1	2	3	4	5	6
7	8	9	10	11	12	13
14	**15**	16	17	18	19	20
21	22	23	24	25	26	27
28						

MARCH

S	M	T	W	T	F	S
	1	2	3	4	5	6
7	8	9	10	11	12	13
14	15	16	17	18	19	20
21	22	23	24	25	26	27
28	29	30	31			

APRIL

S	M	T	W	T	F	S
				1	**2**	3
4	**5**	6	7	8	9	10
11	12	13	14	15	16	17
18	19	20	21	22	23	24
25	26	27	28	29	30	

MAY

S	M	T	W	T	F	S
						1
2	3	4	5	6	7	8
9	10	11	12	13	14	15
16	17	18	19	20	21	22
23	**24**	25	26	27	28	29
30	**31**					

JUNE

S	M	T	W	T	F	S
		1	2	3	4	5
6	7	8	9	10	11	12
13	14	15	16	17	18	19
20	21	22	23	24	25	26
27	28	29	30			

JULY

S	M	T	W	T	F	S
				1	2	3
4	5	6	7	8	9	10
11	12	13	14	15	16	17
18	19	20	21	22	23	24
25	26	27	28	29	30	31

AUGUST

S	M	T	W	T	F	S
1	2	3	4	5	6	7
8	9	10	11	12	13	14
15	16	17	18	19	20	21
22	23	24	25	26	27	28
29	30	31				

SEPTEMBER

S	M	T	W	T	F	S
			1	2	3	4
5	**6**	7	8	9	10	11
12	13	14	15	16	17	18
19	20	21	22	23	24	25
26	27	28	29	30		

OCTOBER

S	M	T	W	T	F	S
					1	2
3	4	5	6	7	8	9
10	**11**	12	13	14	15	16
17	18	19	20	21	22	23
24	25	26	27	28	29	30
31						

NOVEMBER

S	M	T	W	T	F	S
	1	2	3	4	5	6
7	8	9	10	**11**	12	13
14	15	16	17	18	19	20
21	22	23	24	**25**	26	27
28	29	30				

DECEMBER

S	M	T	W	T	F	S
			1	2	3	4
5	6	7	8	9	10	11
12	13	14	15	16	17	18
19	20	21	22	23	24	**25**
26	27	28	29	30	31	

Look ahead with the 2022/2023 Advance Planners at the back of this calendar.

125 Years Ago

January 1896

While it is a good plan to have faith in Providence, it is a bad plan to sit in the easy-chair and wait for Providence to pull the weeds and cultivate the soil among the garden crops.

–The Old Farmer's Almanac

**JANUARY 28:
FULL WOLF MOON**

The last 12 days of January rule the weather for the whole year.

To read a poem in January is as lovely as to go for a walk in June.

–Jean-Paul Sartre, French philosopher (1905–80)

–David Shankbone/Wikimedia

12 Facts About the Number 21

In the early hours of January 1, 1930, Jack Kriendler and Charlie Berns opened their "21 Club," a speakeasy/restaurant named for its address at 21 West 52nd Street in New York City. Known simply as "21," it featured good food, a secret wine cellar, and celebrity patrons who made it an institution. It's said that more business deals are made at "21" than on the floor of the New York Stock Exchange.

THE MONTH OF JANUARY

SUNDAY	MONDAY	TUESDAY	WEDNESDAY	THURSDAY	FRIDAY	SATURDAY
					1	2
3	4	5	6	7	8	9
10	11	12	13	14	15	16
17	18	19	20	21	22	23
24 / 31	25	26	27	28	29	30

For this month's holidays and Moon phases, see the weekly calendar pages that follow.

December 2020 ❧ January 2021

28 *Monday*

Toss your natural Christmas tree into the woods to serve as shelter for birds.

29 *Tuesday*

FULL COLD MOON

30 *Wednesday*

Victorians believed that it was luckiest to marry on the groom's birthday.

31 *Thursday*

The song title "Auld Lang Syne" translates literally as "old long since" but can be understood as "old time's sake."

DECEMBER • 2020							JANUARY • 2021						
S	M	T	W	T	F	S	S	M	T	W	T	F	S
		1	2	3	4	5						1	2
6	7	8	9	10	11	12	3	4	5	6	7	8	9
13	14	15	16	17	18	19	10	11	12	13	14	15	16
20	21	22	23	24	25	26	17	18	19	20	21	22	23
27	28	29	30	31			24	25	26	27	28	29	30
							31						

Friday

1

New Year's Day

I hear you, blithe new year, ring out your laughter
And promises so sweet!

–Abba Goold Woolson, American poet (1838–1921)

Saturday

2

Over the past four decades, the fastest-growing segment of the commercial real estate market has been off-site storage.

Sunday

3

After a dinner party, offer your guests anise seeds; they can be chewed to aid digestion and freshen breath.

REMINDERS

....
....
....
....
....
....

January

4 *Monday*

The name "chicken pox" may have come from the Old English term "gican pox," which means "itching pox."

5 *Tuesday*

Invert a heated bowl over butter to soften it.

6 *Wednesday*

LAST QUARTER

Epiphany

7 *Thursday*

On this day in 1978, Emilio Maros de Palma was born at an Argentine base in Antarctica. His birth was the first on that continent and the southernmost in history.

JANUARY • 2021							FEBRUARY • 2021						
S	M	T	W	T	F	S	S	M	T	W	T	F	S
					1	2		1	2	3	4	5	6
3	4	5	6	7	8	9	7	8	9	10	11	12	13
10	11	12	13	14	15	16	14	15	16	17	18	19	20
17	18	19	20	21	22	23	21	22	23	24	25	26	27
24	25	26	27	28	29	30	28						
31													

Friday 8

Elvis Presley's Birthday

A good head and a good heart are always a formidable combination.

–Nelson Mandela, South African statesman (1918–2013)

Saturday 9

In donkey terms, a jack is a male and a jenny is a female.

Sunday 10

To attract birds, roll a pinecone in honey and then birdseed and hang it on a tree.

REMINDERS

January

11 *Monday*

On this day in 1980, Chinook winds raised the temperature in Great Falls, Montana, from –32° to 15°F in 7 minutes.

12 *Tuesday*

A CLOSE SHAVE
Scientists believe that early humans removed unwanted hair by shaving with clamshells or flint razors.

13 *Wednesday*

NEW MOON

14 *Thursday*

Pitter, patter, slush and splatter, Snowmen shrink and then grow fatter!
–The Old Farmer's Almanac, 2006

JANUARY • 2021							FEBRUARY • 2021						
S	M	T	W	T	F	S	S	M	T	W	T	F	S
					1	2		1	2	3	4	5	6
3	4	5	6	7	8	9	7	8	9	10	11	12	13
10	11	12	13	14	15	16	14	15	16	17	18	19	20
17	18	19	20	21	22	23	21	22	23	24	25	26	27
24	25	26	27	28	29	30	28						
31													

Friday 15

SPOONERISMS
Named for William A. Spooner (1844–1930), spoonerisms are usually the transposition of initial sounds or letters of two or more words, e.g., a "blushing crow" instead of "a crushing blow."

Saturday 16

About 43 million U.S. jobs are connected in some way to agriculture.

Sunday 17

Benjamin Franklin's Birthday

An excellent swimmer, Benjamin Franklin invented swim fins for his hands.

REMINDERS

How cold will it be? Get your local forecast at Almanac.com.

January

18 *Monday*

*Only in the darkness
can you see the stars.*
–Martin Luther King Jr., American
civil rights leader (1929–68)

19 *Tuesday*

In 1990, astronaut
Roberta Bondar became
the first Canadian
woman selected for a
space mission.

20 *Wednesday*

FIRST QUARTER

Inauguration Day

21 *Thursday*

To remove the smell
of onions from
your hands, rub them
with dry mustard
and then wash.

JANUARY • 2021	FEBRUARY • 2021
S M T W T F S	S M T W T F S
1 2	1 2 3 4 5 6
3 4 5 6 7 8 9	7 8 9 10 11 12 13
10 11 12 13 14 15 16	14 15 16 17 18 19 20
17 18 19 20 21 22 23	21 22 23 24 25 26 27
24 25 26 27 28 29 30	28
31	

Friday **22**

If the Sun shines on
St. Vincent's day (today),
a fine crop of grapes
may be expected.

Saturday **23**

Knowledge is
madness if good sense
does not direct it.
–Spanish proverb

Sunday **24**

HIC, HIC, HOORAY!
The *Oxford
English Dictionary*
contains more than
20 different
spellings of the
word "hiccup,"
some going back
to 1544.

REMINDERS

....

....

....

....

....

....

January

25 *Monday*

Mondays are propitious for peace and reconciliation.

26 *Tuesday*

Zero Seconds Rule: Discard any food that falls onto the floor. Bacteria can be transferred to it immediately upon contact.

27 *Wednesday*

Wolves have only one breeding season— late winter.

28 *Thursday*

FULL WOLF MOON

		JANUARY • 2021								FEBRUARY • 2021				

S	M	T	W	T	F	S		S	M	T	W	T	F	S
					1	2			1	2	3	4	5	6
3	4	5	6	7	8	9		7	8	9	10	11	12	13
10	11	12	13	14	15	16		14	15	16	17	18	19	20
17	18	19	20	21	22	23		21	22	23	24	25	26	27
24	25	26	27	28	29	30		28						
31														

Friday **29**

People don't notice whether it's winter or summer when they're happy.
–Anton Chekhov, Russian playwright (1860–1904)

Saturday **30**

Q: What do you call a bee with a low buzz?

A: A mumble bee.

Sunday **31**

According to a recent study, one in seven parents admits that a "terrible mistake" was made in the name that they chose for their child.

REMINDERS

125 Years Ago

February 1896

Window plants during cold weather should be watered with tepid water. . . . While some plants in the sitting room are very desirable, there should never be so many as to shut out the light and sunshine.

–The Old Farmer's Almanac

**FEBRUARY 27:
FULL SNOW MOON**

–Roger Trentham/Getty Images

It is better to see
a pack of wolves than
a fine February.

*Come when the rains
Have glazed the snow and clothed the trees with ice,
While the slant sun of February pours
Into the bowers a flood of light.*

–William Cullen Bryant, American poet (1794–1878)

21   44.956

Sc

Scandium

$[Ar]\ 3d^1 4s^2$

Transition Metals

12 Facts About the Number 21

Scandium, the element with atomic number 21, is used in high-intensity lighting for television and movies, to make solid oxide fuel cells, and in alloys for everything from baseball bats to Russian fighter planes.

THE MONTH OF FEBRUARY

SUNDAY	MONDAY	TUESDAY	WEDNESDAY	THURSDAY	FRIDAY	SATURDAY
	1	2	3	4	5	6
7	8	9	10	11	12	13
14	15	16	17	18	19	20
21	22	23	24	25	26	27
28						

For this month's holidays and Moon phases, see the weekly calendar pages that follow.

February

1 Monday

*Though February is
short, it is filled
with lots of love and
sweet surprises.*
–attributed to Charmaine J. Forde

2 Tuesday

Candlemas
Groundhog Day

*Groundhogs see the
Sun, then duck it;
Milder now, but
pouring buckets!*
–The Old Farmer's Almanac, 2006

3 Wednesday

About 26 percent
of U.S. pets have had
massages, physical
therapy, chiropractic,
or acupuncture.

4 Thursday

LAST QUARTER

FEBRUARY • 2021

S	M	T	W	T	F	S
	1	2	3	4	5	6
7	8	9	10	11	12	13
14	15	16	17	18	19	20
21	22	23	24	25	26	27
28						

MARCH • 2021

S	M	T	W	T	F	S
	1	2	3	4	5	6
7	8	9	10	11	12	13
14	15	16	17	18	19	20
21	22	23	24	25	26	27
28	29	30	31			

FEBRUARY

Friday 5

According to folklore, leaving your shoes with the toes pointing east will forestall nightmares.

Saturday 6

On this day in 1971, Alan Shepard became the first man to hit a golf ball on the Moon. He shanked it.

Sunday 7

To help prevent pain in your lower back, put a footrest under your desk.

REMINDERS

February

8 *Monday*

Never answer an anonymous letter.

–Yogi Berra, American baseball
player (1925–2015)

9 *Tuesday*

Check garden
bulbs in storage and
discard any that
are rotten.

10 *Wednesday*

Chionophobia
is the fear of snow.

11 *Thursday*

NEW MOON

FEBRUARY • 2021	MARCH • 2021
S M T W T F S	S M T W T F S
1 2 3 4 5 6	1 2 3 4 5 6
7 8 9 10 11 12 13	7 8 9 10 11 12 13
14 15 16 17 18 19 20	14 15 16 17 18 19 20
21 22 23 24 25 26 27	21 22 23 24 25 26 27
28	28 29 30 31

Friday 12

Abraham Lincoln's Birthday

Chinese New Year
(Year of the Ox)

A CLOSE SHAVE
Abraham Lincoln was
the first U.S. president
to have a full beard.

Saturday 13

*The most important
thing about skating is
that it teaches
you to do the things
that you should do
before you do the
things you want to do.*
–Barbara Ann Scott, Canadian
figure skater (1928–2012)

Sunday 14

Valentine's Day

St. Valentine is the
patron saint
of beekeepers as
well as love.

R E M I N D E R S

....

....

....

....

....

Make it all chocolate, all the time, with recipes from Almanac.com.

February

15   *Monday*

Presidents' Day
National Flag of Canada Day
Susan B. Anthony's
Birthday (Fla.)
Family Day
(Alta., B.C., N.B., Ont., Sask.)
Great minds think alike.

16   *Tuesday*

Mardi Gras (Ala., La.)
**The state crustacean
of Louisiana
is the crawfish.**

17   *Wednesday*

𝔄𝔰𝔥 𝔚𝔢𝔡𝔫𝔢𝔰𝔡𝔞𝔶
**Christians traditionally
fast on this first
day of Lent, with some
continuing throughout
the entire Lenten
season.**

18   *Thursday*

**SPOONERISMS
TV announcer:
"All the world was
thrilled by the marriage
of the Duck and
Doochess of Windsor."**

FEBRUARY • 2021	MARCH • 2021
S M T W T F S	S M T W T F S
1 2 3 4 5 6	1 2 3 4 5 6
7 8 9 10 11 12 13	7 8 9 10 11 12 13
14 15 16 17 18 19 20	14 15 16 17 18 19 20
21 22 23 24 25 26 27	21 22 23 24 25 26 27
28	28 29 30 31

FEBRUARY

Friday **19**

FIRST QUARTER

Saturday **20**

It is lucky to put on
an apron inside out.

Sunday **21**

The Sun is about
400,000 times brighter
than the full Moon.

REMINDERS

....
....
....
....
....

Make it all chocolate, all the time, with recipes from Almanac.com.

February

22 Monday

George Washington's Birthday

At his Mount Vernon plantation, George Washington operated a commercial distillery, where some of his crops were used to create whiskey.

23 Tuesday

On this day in 1921, the first coast-to-coast U.S. airmail was delivered to New York from San Francisco.

24 Wednesday

To know one's self is the true; to strive with one's self is the good; to conquer one's self is the beautiful.

–Joseph Roux,
French priest (1834–86)

25 Thursday

HIC, HIC, HOORAY! According to folklore, lifting up one side of a rock and spitting underneath it will cure hiccups.

FEBRUARY • 2021						
S	M	T	W	T	F	S
	1	2	3	4	5	6
7	8	9	10	11	12	13
14	15	16	17	18	19	20
21	22	23	24	25	26	27
28						

MARCH • 2021						
S	M	T	W	T	F	S
	1	2	3	4	5	6
7	8	9	10	11	12	13
14	15	16	17	18	19	20
21	22	23	24	25	26	27
28	29	30	31			

Friday 26

Heritage Day (Y.T.)

About 4 percent of
Canadians who grow
fruit, herbs, vegetables,
or flowers do so in
community gardens.

Saturday 27

FULL SNOW MOON

Sunday 28

On this day in 2001,
a magnitude 6.8
earthquake shook the
Nisqually Valley near
Olympia, Washington.

REMINDERS

....
....
....
....
....

Make it all chocolate, all the time, with recipes from Almanac.com.

125 Years Ago

March 1896

Success in farming depends very much on being ready to do everything at the right time. To be always two weeks behind time is to invite failure.

–*The Old Farmer's Almanac*

**MARCH 28:
FULL WORM MOON**

March comes in with adders' heads and goes out with peacocks' tails.

In March, the soft rains continued, and each storm waited courteously until its predecessor had sunk beneath the ground.

–John Steinbeck, American writer (1902–68)

–Tatiana Dyuvbanova/Getty Images

12 Facts About the Number 21

March 21 is World Down Syndrome Day. Also called trisomy 21 (referring to the condition of having three copies of chromosome 21 instead of a pair), Down Syndrome is a genetic disorder that affects development, resulting in both physical and mental challenges. It was first fully described by British doctor John Langdon Down in 1866. Today, the condition affects more than 6 million individuals worldwide.

THE MONTH OF MARCH

SUNDAY	MONDAY	TUESDAY	WEDNESDAY	THURSDAY	FRIDAY	SATURDAY
	1	2	3	4	5	6
7	8	9	10	11	12	13
14	15	16	17	18	19	20
21	22	23	24	25	26	27
28	29	30	31			

For this month's holidays and Moon phases, see the weekly calendar pages that follow.

March

1 *Monday*

Folklore advises that you not carry furniture into a new house until the salt and pepper are on the shelf.

2 *Tuesday*

Texas Independence Day
Town Meeting Day (Vt.)

In its 2019 Town Meeting, the voters of Fair Haven, Vermont, elected a Nubian goat named Lincoln as honorary mayor.

3 *Wednesday*

If you sneeze while eating at a table, you will have a new friend before the next meal.

4 *Thursday*

On this day in 1809, the first U.S. presidential inaugural ball took place, with President James Madison's wife, Dolley, serving as hostess.

	MARCH • 2021							APRIL • 2021					
S	M	T	W	T	F	S	S	M	T	W	T	F	S
	1	2	3	4	5	6					1	2	3
7	8	9	10	11	12	13	4	5	6	7	8	9	10
14	15	16	17	18	19	20	11	12	13	14	15	16	17
21	22	23	24	25	26	27	18	19	20	21	22	23	24
28	29	30	31				25	26	27	28	29	30	

Friday

5

LAST QUARTER

Lightning may
take the form of
grapefruit-size balls
of fire that roll
along the ground.

Saturday

6

A bag of chips
usually contains about
43 percent air.

Sunday

7

REMINDERS

....

....

....

....

....

....

MARCH

March

8 Monday

International Women's Day
Commonwealth Day
(Canada)

***With the new day
comes new strength
and new thoughts.***
–Eleanor Roosevelt,
U.S. First Lady (1884–1962)

9 Tuesday

Hummingbirds
migrate north now.

10 Wednesday

A CLOSE SHAVE
Viking burial mounds
from 1500 to 1200 B.C.
contain bronze
razors shaped like
horse heads.

11 Thursday

Q: Did you hear about
the two silkworms
that had a race?
A: It ended in a tie.

MARCH • 2021								APRIL • 2021					
S	M	T	W	T	F	S		S	M	T	W	T	F	S
	1	2	3	4	5	6						1	2	3
7	8	9	10	11	12	13		4	5	6	7	8	9	10
14	15	16	17	18	19	20		11	12	13	14	15	16	17
21	22	23	24	25	26	27		18	19	20	21	22	23	24
28	29	30	31					25	26	27	28	29	30	

Friday **12**

To grow rich, look at the new Moon (tomorrow) with money in your hands.

Saturday **13**

NEW MOON

Sunday **14**

Daylight Saving Time begins at 2:00 A.M.

Time is what prevents everything from happening at once.
–John Archibald Wheeler, American physicist (1911–2008)

REMINDERS

....
....
....
....
....
....

Spring returns! Get your garden ready at Almanac.com.

March

15 *Monday*

Clean Monday

In Greece, Clean Monday, which marks the beginning of Great Lent for Orthodox Christians, is also considered the traditional start of kite-flying season.

16 *Tuesday*

On this day in 1926, American scientist Robert Hutchings Goddard launched the world's first liquid-fueled rocket. The flight lasted 2 seconds and reached an altitude of 41 feet.

17 *Wednesday*

St. Patrick's Day

Evacuation Day (Suffolk Co., Mass.)

In Irish folklore, leprechauns are often depicted as being cobblers for the fairy world.

18 *Thursday*

SPOONERISMS
"A half-warmed fish" unscrambled is "a half-formed wish."

MARCH • 2021	APRIL • 2021
S M T W T F S	S M T W T F S
1 2 3 4 5 6	1 2 3
7 8 9 10 11 12 13	4 5 6 7 8 9 10
14 15 16 17 18 19 20	11 12 13 14 15 16 17
21 22 23 24 25 26 27	18 19 20 21 22 23 24
28 29 30 31	25 26 27 28 29 30

Friday 19

On this day in 2018, Sudan, the last male white rhino, died in Kenya.

Saturday 20

Vernal Equinox

*Spring! The beautiful
Spring is coming,
The Sun shines bright
and the bees
are humming.*

–Mary Howitt,
English poet (1799–1888)

Sunday 21

FIRST QUARTER

Reminders

....
....
....
....
....
....

Spring returns! Get your garden ready at Almanac.com.

March

22 Monday

When black snails on
the road you see,
Then on the morrow
rain will be.

23 Tuesday

On this day in 2001,
the Russian space
station *Mir* ended
15 years in space
by plunging into the
Pacific Ocean.

24 Wednesday

*Let others praise
ancient times;
I am glad I was
born in these.*
–Ovid, Roman poet
(43 B.C.–A.D. 17)

25 Thursday

HIC, HIC, HOORAY!
To cure hiccups,
folklore advises to
pant like a dog.

MARCH • 2021

S	M	T	W	T	F	S
	1	2	3	4	5	6
7	8	9	10	11	12	13
14	15	16	17	18	19	20
21	22	23	24	25	26	27
28	29	30	31			

APRIL • 2021

S	M	T	W	T	F	S
				1	2	3
4	5	6	7	8	9	10
11	12	13	14	15	16	17
18	19	20	21	22	23	24
25	26	27	28	29	30	

MARCH

Friday 26

Break an egg, break your leg;
  Break three, woe to thee;
Break two, your love is true.

Saturday 27

Passover begins at sundown

It is a Jewish tradition
to dispose of all
chametz (leaven or
leaven-based items)
before Passover.

Sunday 28

FULL WORM MOON

Palm Sunday

REMINDERS

....
....
....
....
....

Spring returns! Get your garden ready at Almanac.com.

March ❧ April

29 Monday

30 Tuesday

To avoid selenium toxicity, don't eat Brazil nuts daily: Just one nut can provide about 124 to 165 percent of the recommended dietary allowance (RDA) of selenium.

31 Wednesday

César Chávez Day

To make a great dream come true, the first requirement is a great capacity to dream; the second is persistence.

–César Chávez, American labor leader (1927–93)

1 Thursday

All Fools' Day

Q: Who invented fractions?

A: Henry the 1/8.

MARCH • 2021

S	M	T	W	T	F	S
	1	2	3	4	5	6
7	8	9	10	11	12	13
14	15	16	17	18	19	20
21	22	23	24	25	26	27
28	29	30	31			

APRIL • 2021

S	M	T	W	T	F	S
				1	2	3
4	5	6	7	8	9	10
11	12	13	14	15	16	17
18	19	20	21	22	23	24
25	26	27	28	29	30	

MAR/APR

Good Friday
Pascua Florida Day

Friday

2

The Everglades in southern Florida are the only place where American alligators and American crocodiles coexist.

O truly blessed night, when things of heaven are wed to those of earth, and divine to the human.

–English translation of "The Exsultet," a Roman Catholic hymn of rejoicing sung on Easter eve

Saturday

3

Sunday

4

LAST QUARTER

Easter

REMINDERS

....
....
....
....
....
....

Spring returns! Get your garden ready at Almanac.com.

125 Years Ago

April 1896

The early garden needs attention as soon as the frost is well out of the ground. Peas should be among the first vegetables to be planted. Select a warm, sunny location; follow with radishes, turnips, beets, onion sets, and early corn.

—The Old Farmer's Almanac

APRIL 26
FULL PINK MOON

A cold April
The barn will fill.

*Here cometh April again,
and as far as I can see, the world hath
more fools in it than ever.*

–Charles Lamb, English essayist (1775–1834)

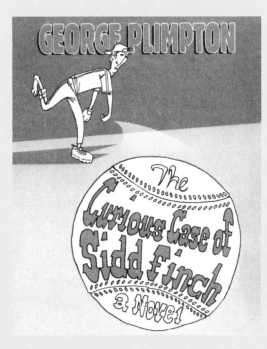

12 Facts About the Number 21

21 was the uniform number of Sidd Finch, a rookie baseball pitcher said to be capable of throwing a 168-mph fastball thanks to his training as a yogi. His story, "reported" by George Plimpton, appeared in the April 1, 1985, issue of *Sports Illustrated* and turned out to be one of the best-known April Fools' Day hoaxes in sports history.

THE MONTH OF APRIL

SUNDAY	MONDAY	TUESDAY	WEDNESDAY	THURSDAY	FRIDAY	SATURDAY
				1	2	3
4	5	6	7	8	9	10
11	12	13	14	15	16	17
18	19	20	21	22	23	24
25	26	27	28	29	30	

For this month's holidays and Moon phases, see the weekly calendar pages that follow.

April

5 Monday

Easter Monday

Attention skywatchers: Utah's Natural Bridges National Monument, the world's first International Dark Sky Park, rates a 2 on the 9-point Bortle system (1 is completely dark).

6 Tuesday

If bird droppings land on you, it is said that good luck will come your way.

7 Wednesday

If you used tree wrap to protect young trees from sunscald this past winter, remove it in early April to avoid girdling and to discourage insects and diseases.

8 Thursday

A farmer's life is the life for me, I own I love it dearly; And every season, full of glee, I take its labours cheerly.

–song by J. J. Barker sung at a meeting of the Agricultural Society in New Brunswick, April 1821

APRIL • 2021

S M T W T F S

				1	2	3
4	5	6	7	8	9	10
11	12	13	14	15	16	17
18	19	20	21	22	23	24
25	26	27	28	29	30	

MAY • 2021

S M T W T F S

						1
2	3	4	5	6	7	8
9	10	11	12	13	14	15
16	17	18	19	20	21	22
23	24	25	26	27	28	29
30	31					

Friday

9

Add spices to chicken soup to intensify its healing powers: Garlic may help to kill viruses and bacteria, while cayenne and black pepper can act as expectorants.

APRIL

Saturday

10

After receiving an unexpected invitation from the People's Republic of China, a U.S. table tennis team began a tour of the country on this day in 1971, initiating "Ping-Pong diplomacy."

Sunday

11

NEW MOON

REMINDERS

....

....

....

....

....

....

April

12 Monday

To encourage
growth, prune shrubs
between the new
and full Moons.

13 Tuesday

Thomas Jefferson's Birthday

*Give up money, give
up fame, give up
science, give up the
earth itself and all it
contains, rather than
do an immoral act.*

–excerpt from letter by Thomas
Jefferson to Peter Carr, 1785

14 Wednesday

The early bird might
get the worm, but the second
mouse gets the cheese.

15 Thursday

A CLOSE SHAVE
Clean-shaven Alexander
the Great encouraged
his soldiers to follow
his example, so that
enemies could not grab
them by the beard.

APRIL • 2021							MAY • 2021						
S	M	T	W	T	F	S	S	M	T	W	T	F	S
				1	2	3							1
4	5	6	7	8	9	10	2	3	4	5	6	7	8
11	12	13	14	15	16	17	9	10	11	12	13	14	15
18	19	20	21	22	23	24	16	17	18	19	20	21	22
25	26	27	28	29	30		23	24	25	26	27	28	29
							30	31					

APRIL

Friday **16**

According to one study, over the course of our lifetime we spend a total of 3,680 hours (153 days) searching for misplaced items.

Saturday **17**

On the way to your wedding, it is good luck to meet a chimney sweep, elephant, or toad. (Or a chimney sweep with a toad in his pocket riding an elephant.)

Sunday **18**

SPOONERISMS
"Noble tons of soil" unscrambled is "Noble sons of toil."

REMINDERS

....
....
....
....
....

April

19 Monday

Patriots Day (Maine, Mass.)

Here once the embattled farmers stood, And fired the shot heard 'round the world.

–"Concord Hymn,"
by Ralph Waldo Emerson,
American writer (1803–82)

20 Tuesday

FIRST QUARTER

21 Wednesday

San Jacinto Day (Tex.)

On this day in 1836, Sam Houston's small army of Texans defeated General Santa Anna's larger Mexican force. The Texan battle cry of the day was "Remember the Alamo!"

22 Thursday

Earth Day

The ultimate test of man's conscience may be his willingness to sacrifice something today for future generations whose words of thanks will not be heard.

–Gaylord Nelson, U.S. senator
and founder of Earth Day
(1916–2005)

APRIL • 2021							MAY • 2021						
S	M	T	W	T	F	S	S	M	T	W	T	F	S
				1	2	3							1
4	5	6	7	8	9	10	2	3	4	5	6	7	8
11	12	13	14	15	16	17	9	10	11	12	13	14	15
18	19	20	21	22	23	24	16	17	18	19	20	21	22
25	26	27	28	29	30		23	24	25	26	27	28	29
							30	31					

Friday **23**

William Shakespeare is thought to have both been born (1564) and died (1616) on this day.

APRIL

Saturday **24**

Birthday of Robert B. Thomas, founder of *The Old Farmer's Alamanc*

A Sumerian clay tablet from around 1700 to 1500 B.C. is the earliest known farmers' almanac.

Sunday **25**

HIC, HIC, HOORAY! To cure hiccups, eat a spoonful of peanut butter.

REMINDERS

....
....
....
....
....
....

April May

26 *Monday*

FULL PINK MOON

St. George's Day,
observed (N.L.)

27 *Tuesday*

At sunset with a
cloud so black,
A westerly wind you
shall not lack.

28 *Wednesday*

The secret of patience:
Do something else.

29 *Thursday*

To cure a toothache, folklore
advises to kiss a donkey.

APRIL • 2021

S	M	T	W	T	F	S
				1	2	3
4	5	6	7	8	9	10
11	12	13	14	15	16	17
18	19	20	21	22	23	24
25	26	27	28	29	30	

MAY • 2021

S	M	T	W	T	F	S
						1
2	3	4	5	6	7	8
9	10	11	12	13	14	15
16	17	18	19	20	21	22
23	24	25	26	27	28	29
30	31					

APR/MAY

National Arbor Day

Friday 30

"Moon" trees, five species grown from hundreds of seeds that had orbited the Moon in 1971, were planted across the globe, including a loblolly pine at the White House.

May Day

Saturday 1

For long-lasting blooms, pick flowers in the late afternoon, when the leaves and stems contain the most sugar.

Orthodox Easter

Sunday 2

Joy is the emotional expression of the courageous Yes to one's own true being.

–Paul Tillich, German-born American theologian and philosopher (1886–1965)

REMINDERS

....

....

....

....

....

....

Will April bring showers? Check your local forecast at Almanac.com.

May
with The Old Farmer's Almanac

125 Years Ago

May 1896

This is the farmer's busy month—plowing, planting, hoeing, and killing worms, bugs, and the whole tribe of biting insects which threaten to destroy his crops.

—The Old Farmer's Almanac

**MAY 26
FULL FLOWER MOON**

Mud in May,
grain in August.

*Spring has returned.
The Earth is like a child who knows poems.*
–Rainer Maria Rilke, German poet (1875–1926)

–Stocktrek Images/Getty Images

12 Facts About the Number 21

● "21 guns" is a military salute performed to recognize the U.S. national flag, visiting royalty, and foreign heads of state. It is also fired at military installations at noon on Memorial Day, as well as used to honor the U.S. president, president-elect, and ex-president(s), both in the present and at noon on the day of their funeral.

● In Canada, such salutes are fired for the sovereign, members of the royal family, the governor-general, and foreign heads of state and members of foreign reigning royal families, as well as on Canada Day and Remembrance Day.

THE MONTH OF MAY

SUNDAY	MONDAY	TUESDAY	WEDNESDAY	THURSDAY	FRIDAY	SATURDAY
						1
2	3	4	5	6	7	8
9	10	11	12	13	14	15
16	17	18	19	20	21	22
23	24	25	26	27	28	29
30	31					

For this month's holidays and Moon phases, see the weekly calendar pages that follow.

May

3 Monday

LAST QUARTER

4 Tuesday

Save chopsticks from take-out restaurants. They make great stakes for smaller plants.

5 Wednesday

Cinco de Mayo

It is not enough to know how to ride; you must also know how to fall.

–Mexican proverb

6 Thursday

On this day in 1915, Babe Ruth of the Boston Red Sox hit his first major league home run in a game against the New York Yankees.

MAY • 2021							JUNE • 2021						
S	M	T	W	T	F	S	S	M	T	W	T	F	S
						1			1	2	3	4	5
2	3	4	5	6	7	8	6	7	8	9	10	11	12
9	10	11	12	13	14	15	13	14	15	16	17	18	19
16	17	18	19	20	21	22	20	21	22	23	24	25	26
23	24	25	26	27	28	29	27	28	29	30			
30	31												

Friday **7**

Condition your
hair with mayonnaise
to make it soft
and shiny.

Truman Day (Mo.)

Saturday **8**

*Not all readers
are leaders, but all
leaders are readers.*

–Harry Truman, 33rd U.S.
president (1884–1972)

Mother's Day

Sunday **9**

On Mother's Day
in Peru, families honor
mothers both present
and deceased.

MAY

REMINDERS

....
....
....
....
....

May

10 *Monday*

*A bird doesn't sing
because it has
an answer; it sings
because it has a song.*

–Maya Angelou,
American writer (1928–2014)

11 *Tuesday*

NEW MOON

12 *Wednesday*

The eye that
sees all things else
sees not itself.

13 *Thursday*

Today begins the 4-day
Jumping Frog Jubilee
in Angels Camp,
California, the setting
of Mark Twain's 1865
story, "The Celebrated
Jumping Frog of
Calaveras County."

MAY • 2021							JUNE • 2021						
S	M	T	W	T	F	S	S	M	T	W	T	F	S
						1			1	2	3	4	5
2	3	4	5	6	7	8	6	7	8	9	10	11	12
9	10	11	12	13	14	15	13	14	15	16	17	18	19
16	17	18	19	20	21	22	20	21	22	23	24	25	26
23	24	25	26	27	28	29	27	28	29	30			
30	31												

Friday **14**

On this day in 1804,
the Lewis and Clark
expedition started
from Camp River
Dubois, near present
day Hartford, Illinois.

Saturday **15**

Armed Forces Day

*The battle, sir, is not to
the strong alone;
it is to the vigilant, the
active, the brave.*

–Patrick Henry, American
statesman (1736–99)

MAY

Sunday **16**

A CLOSE SHAVE
Ancient Egyptian
nobles shaved their
heads and bodies,
but men (and
women pharaohs)
sometimes wore
false beards.

REMINDERS

....
....
....
....
....
....

May

17 *Monday*

Due to emerge from the ground this year in 15 states, Brood X, aka the Great Eastern Brood, is the largest group of 17-year locusts.

18 *Tuesday*

SPOONERISMS
"You hissed my mystery lectures" unscrambled is "You missed my history lectures."

19 *Wednesday*

FIRST QUARTER

20 *Thursday*

The Sun makes up 99.86 percent of our solar system's mass.

MAY • 2021

S	M	T	W	T	F	S
						1
2	3	4	5	6	7	8
9	10	11	12	13	14	15
16	17	18	19	20	21	22
23	24	25	26	27	28	29
30	31					

JUNE • 2021

S	M	T	W	T	F	S
		1	2	3	4	5
6	7	8	9	10	11	12
13	14	15	16	17	18	19
20	21	22	23	24	25	26
27	28	29	30			

Friday **21**

*Lettuce is like
conversation: It must
be fresh and crisp,
so sparkling that
you scarcely notice
the bitter in it.*
–Charles Dudley Warner,
American editor (1829–1900)

Saturday **22**

MAY

National Maritime Day

During the age of sail,
some sailors believed
that whistling in
times of calm might
bring much-needed
wind, but if not done
correctly, risked
generating too much.

Sunday **23**

Whitsunday—Pentecost

"Dust" curtains
by placing them in
the dryer on "Air Fluff"
for a few minutes.

REMINDERS

....
....
....
....
....
....

May

24 *Monday*

You should address a British queen as "Your Majesty" when you are first introduced. In further conversation, use "Ma'am." Introduce her to others as "Her Majesty the Queen."

25 *Tuesday*

Q: How does the man on the Moon cut his hair?

A: Eclipse it.

26 *Wednesday*

FULL FLOWER MOON

Total Lunar Eclipse (visible in parts of N.Am.)

27 *Thursday*

HIC, HIC, HOORAY! To cure hiccups, drink water while bending over.

MAY • 2021							JUNE • 2021						
S	M	T	W	T	F	S	S	M	T	W	T	F	S
						1			1	2	3	4	5
2	3	4	5	6	7	8	6	7	8	9	10	11	12
9	10	11	12	13	14	15	13	14	15	16	17	18	19
16	17	18	19	20	21	22	20	21	22	23	24	25	26
23	24	25	26	27	28	29	27	28	29	30			
30	31												

Friday 28

You are considered
lucky if the initials
of your full name
spell a word.

Saturday 29

MAY

Mopping floors and
fishing both burn
approximately 0.028
of a calorie per
minute per pound
of body weight.

Sunday 30

*The fixity of a habit
is generally in
direct proportion to
its absurdity.*
–Marcel Proust,
French writer (1871–1922)

REMINDERS

....
....
....
....
....
....

125 Years Ago

June 1896

The weeds that obstruct our progress urge us to activity and spur us on to better things. Thus, the farmer always can find lessons in nature that will lead him to a higher atmosphere of thought.

–The Old Farmer's Almanac

JUNE 24
FULL STRAWBERRY MOON

If it rains on June 27,
it will rain for 7 weeks.

Summer is drawn blinds in Louisiana, long winds in Wyoming, shade of elms and maples in New England.

–Archibald MacLeish, American poet (1892–1982)

–Prostock-Studio/Getty Images

12 Facts About the Number 21

Researchers at The Ohio State University believe that there are 21 basic human facial expressions, not the traditionally believed six.

THE MONTH OF JUNE

SUNDAY	MONDAY	TUESDAY	WEDNESDAY	THURSDAY	FRIDAY	SATURDAY
		1	2	3	4	5
6	7	8	9	10	11	12
13	14	15	16	17	18	19
20	21	22	23	24	25	26
27	28	29	30			

For this month's holidays and Moon phases, see the weekly calendar pages that follow.

May 🌿 June

31 | *Monday*

There are about
200 species of plants
known as poppies.

1 | *Tuesday*

Although the 1956
Summer Olympics was
held in Melbourne,
equestrian events took
place in Stockholm,
Sweden (almost
10,000 miles away),
because Australian
officials refused to lift a
quarantine on horses.

2 | *Wednesday*

LAST QUARTER

3 | *Thursday*

Good and quickly
seldom meet.
–English proverb

MAY • 2021

S	M	T	W	T	F	S
						1
2	3	4	5	6	7	8
9	10	11	12	13	14	15
16	17	18	19	20	21	22
23	24	25	26	27	28	29
30	31					

JUNE • 2021

S	M	T	W	T	F	S
		1	2	3	4	5
6	7	8	9	10	11	12
13	14	15	16	17	18	19
20	21	22	23	24	25	26
27	28	29	30			

Friday

4

According to folklore,
a cure for malaria is to place
a toad under a pot and
walk around it three times.

Saturday

5

World Environment Day

Check your air
conditioner filter each
month and clean or
replace it as needed.
An appliance with
a dirty filter will use
more energy.

MAY/JUN

Sunday

6

About 15 percent
of U.S. weddings
happen at a barn,
farm, or ranch.

REMINDERS

....
....
....
....
....
....

Love to grow veggies? Almanac.com shows you how, from sowing to harvest.

June

7 Monday

Synchronous fireflies *(Photinus carolinus)* emerge in the Great Smoky Mountains at around this time; the unusual flashing patterns during courtship attract many tourists.

8 Tuesday

Q: Milk from what animal is used to make Roquefort cheese?

A: Sheep.

9 Wednesday

The secret of getting ahead is getting started.
—unknown

10 Thursday

NEW MOON

Annular Solar Eclipse (visible in parts of N.Am.)

JUNE • 2021							JULY • 2021						
S	M	T	W	T	F	S	S	M	T	W	T	F	S
		1	2	3	4	5						1	2	3
6	7	8	9	10	11	12	4	5	6	7	8	9	10
13	14	15	16	17	18	19	11	12	13	14	15	16	17
20	21	22	23	24	25	26	18	19	20	21	22	23	24
27	28	29	30				25	26	27	28	29	30	31

Friday 11

King Kamehameha I Day
(Hawaii)

In addition to his other exploits, King Kamehameha I was a famous rider of surfboards.

Saturday 12

A CLOSE SHAVE
Around A.D. 100, Roman emperor Hadrian (famous for his wall) also revived the fashion of growing beards.

JUNE

Sunday 13

On this day in 1920, the U.S. Post Office declared that babies could no longer be delivered by parcel post.

REMINDERS

....
....
....
....
....
....

Love to grow veggies? Almanac.com shows you how, from sowing to harvest.

June

14 *Monday*

Flag Day

In the United States, only a president, governor, or mayor of the District of Columbia can order the national flag to be flown at half-mast.

15 *Tuesday*

The ears of most species of birds are concealed by feathers called "auriculars," which help the avians to hear above the rush of wind while in flight.

16 *Wednesday*

A rainbow's arc is most pronounced when the Sun is close to the horizon.

17 *Thursday*

FIRST QUARTER

Bunker Hill Day
(Suffolk Co., Mass.)

JUNE • 2021						
S	M	T	W	T	F	S
	1	2	3	4	5
6	7	8	9	10	11	12
13	14	15	16	17	18	19
20	21	22	23	24	25	26
27	28	29	30			

JULY • 2021						
S	M	T	W	T	F	S
				1	2	3
4	5	6	7	8	9	10
11	12	13	14	15	16	17
18	19	20	21	22	23	24
25	26	27	28	29	30	31

SPOONERISMS

"It is kisstomary
to cuss the bride"
unscrambled is
"It is customary to
kiss the bride."

Friday 18

Emancipation Day (Tex.)

*. . . I do order and
declare that all
persons held as
slaves within said
designated States, and
parts of States, are,
and henceforward
shall be free.*

–"Emancipation Proclamation," 1863

Saturday 19

Orthodox Pentecost

Summer Solstice

Father's Day

West Virginia Day

No year has two summers.

Sunday 20

REMINDERS

....
....
....
....
....
....

June

21 Monday

Yukon's Old Crow
Flats contain some of
the earliest evidence
of human habitation in
North America.

22 Tuesday

Another name for
"dragonfly" is "devil's
darning needle"
because the insect
was once thought to
sew shut the eyes,
ears, or mouth of a
sleeping child who had
misbehaved.

23 Wednesday

On this day in 1926,
about 8,000 college
applicants were given
an experimental
intelligence test, later
to be called the SAT.

24 Thursday

**FULL STRAWBERRY
MOON**

Get a Free Bonus Gift!

How would you like to receive next year's elegant Engagement Calendar PLUS a FREE BONUS GIFT?!

Plus, receive a **FREE BONUS GIFT** with your order!

The Old Farmer's Almanac Engagement Calendar is your stylish and handy companion that you can count on to manage your daily appointments and activities. It is also an ideal place to record your daily observations and inspirations. Each day offers a little bit of wit or wisdom to enjoy.

Order now to ensure that you have your 2022 calendar when you need it! PLUS, you get a Free Bonus Gift with your order.

Due to mailing requirements, this offer is only available in the United States.

JUNE

Name: _____

Address: _____

_____

City/Town: _____ State: _____ Zip: _____

The Old Farmer's Almanac
PO Box 520
Dublin, NH 03444-0520

Fold along this line. ▲

After cutting this order form out of the book along the vertical dotted line, fold it in half along the horizontal line. Please be sure to either complete the payment information on the order form or enclose a check. Then tape the envelope closed along the three open edges. DO NOT SEND CASH.

Use clear tape on all three open sides to seal completely.

Cut along dotted line. ▶

JUNE • 2021

S	M	T	W	T	F	S
		1	2	3	4	5
6	7	8	9	10	11	12
13	14	15	16	17	18	19
20	21	22	23	24	25	26
27	28	29	30			

JULY • 2021

S	M	T	W	T	F	S
				1	2	3
4	5	6	7	8	9	10
11	12	13	14	15	16	17
18	19	20	21	22	23	24
25	26	27	28	29	30	31

Friday 25

HIC, HIC, HOORAY!
To cure hiccups,
pull on your tongue.

Saturday 26

Only male crickets
chirp, by rubbing their
forewings together.

Sunday 27

It is good luck to throw back
the first fish you catch.

JUNE

REMINDERS

....
....
....
....
....
....

June July

28 *Monday*

According to the American Kennel Club, beagles are the only dog breed to have appeared on every annual AKC list of the 10 most popular dogs.

29 *Tuesday*

Chicken tetrazzini was named for Italian opera singer Luisa Tetrazzini, born on this day in 1871.

30 *Wednesday*

A swarm of bees in June
Is worth a silver spoon.

1 *Thursday*

LAST QUARTER

Canada Day

JUNE • 2021	JULY • 2021
S M T W T F S	S M T W T F S
1 2 3 4 5	1 2 3
6 7 8 9 10 11 12	4 5 6 7 8 9 10
13 14 15 16 17 18 19	11 12 13 14 15 16 17
20 21 22 23 24 25 26	18 19 20 21 22 23 24
27 28 29 30	25 26 27 28 29 30 31

Friday 2

**Many drops
make a shower.**

Dog Days begin.   *Saturday* 3

*Dogs lead a nice life.
You never see a dog
with a wristwatch.*

–George Carlin, American
humorist (1937–2008)

JUN / JUL

Independence Day   *Sunday* 4

*Fire the rockets!
Sing the anthem!
Bring umbrellas
to the beach
and plant them!*

–The Old Farmer's Almanac, 2006

REMINDERS

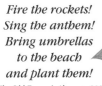

....
....
....
....
....
....

Love to grow veggies? Almanac.com shows you how, from sowing to harvest.

July   with *The Old Farmer's Almanac*

125 Years Ago

July 1896

The farmer has no excuse for letting the weeds grow in July, for improved implements enable him to get his hay so quickly that plenty of time is left to look after the hoed crops.

–*The Old Farmer's Almanac*

JULY 23
FULL BUCK MOON

Ne'er trust a July sky.

We go in withering July
To ply the hard incessant hoe;
Panting beneath the brazen sky
We sweat and grumble, but we go.

–Ruth Pitter, English poet (1897–1992)

–MTA.com

12 Facts About the Number 21

On July 22, 2016, on a single fare, Matthew Ahn visited all 469 of New York City's subway stations then in existence in 21 hours, 28 minutes, and 14 seconds, a world record for the trip.

THE MONTH OF JULY

SUNDAY	MONDAY	TUESDAY	WEDNESDAY	THURSDAY	FRIDAY	SATURDAY
				1	2	3
4	5	6	7	8	9	10
11	12	13	14	15	16	17
18	19	20	21	22	23	24
25	26	27	28	29	30	31

For this month's holidays and Moon phases, see the weekly calendar pages that follow.

July

5 Monday

Fireflies in great numbers indicate fair weather.

6 Tuesday

On this day in 2008, Kent Couch flew across the state of Oregon in a lawn chair attached to balloons.

7 Wednesday

I'll make my joy like this Small Butterfly; Whose happy heart has power To make a stone a flower.
—William Henry Davies, English poet (1871–1940)

8 Thursday

Nobody knows for sure who invented chef's salad, but chef Louis Diat of the Ritz Carlton in New York helped to popularize it in the 1940s.

JULY • 2021							AUGUST • 2021						
S	M	T	W	T	F	S	S	M	T	W	T	F	S
				1	2	3	1	2	3	4	5	6	7
4	5	6	7	8	9	10	8	9	10	11	12	13	14
11	12	13	14	15	16	17	15	16	17	18	19	20	21
18	19	20	21	22	23	24	22	23	24	25	26	27	28
25	26	27	28	29	30	31	29	30	31				

Friday 9

NEW MOON

Nunavut Day (Canada)

Saturday 10

A cat pent up
becomes a lion.
–Italian proverb

Sunday 11

In 1692, the French
word *pique-nique*
first appeared in print.
The English word
"picnic" appeared
later, in 1748.

JULY

REMINDERS

....
....
....
....
....
....

July

12 Monday

Orangemen's Day, (N.L.)

On this day in 2011, Neptune completed its first orbit around the Sun since the planet's discovery in 1846.

13 Tuesday

A CLOSE SHAVE
In the Middle Ages, fashionable European women removed all facial hair, including eyebrows and eyelashes.

14 Wednesday

Dr. Amerson
10:40 AM

118|
70
B.P.

Just because something doesn't do what you planned it to do doesn't mean it's useless.
–Thomas Alva Edison, American inventor (1847–1931)

15 Thursday

Only female mosquitoes bite.

JULY • 2021							AUGUST • 2021						
S	M	T	W	T	F	S	S	M	T	W	T	F	S
				1	2	3	1	2	3	4	5	6	7
4	5	6	7	8	9	10	8	9	10	11	12	13	14
11	12	13	14	15	16	17	15	16	17	18	19	20	21
18	19	20	21	22	23	24	22	23	24	25	26	27	28
25	26	27	28	29	30	31	29	30	31				

Friday 16

One study found that diners who received their bill in a gold folder left an average tip of 21.5 percent, while those whose check arrived in a black folder left 18.9 percent.

Saturday 17

FIRST QUARTER

JULY

Sunday 18

Scientists estimate that a single ragweed plant can release 1 billion grains of pollen over the course of a season.

REMINDERS

....
....
....
....
....

Planning a picnic or party? Get time-saving tips at Almanac.com.

July

19 *Monday*

Hear twice before
you speak once.

20 *Tuesday*

Since Neil Armstrong
and Buzz Aldrin set
foot on the lunar
surface on this day
in 1969, only 10 other
men have walked
on the Moon.

21 *Wednesday*

To minimize watering,
landscape with
plants that are native
to your region.

22 *Thursday*

St. Mary Magdalene

Roses are said to begin
to fade on this day.

JULY • 2021

S	M	T	W	T	F	S
				1	2	3
4	5	6	7	8	9	10
11	12	13	14	15	16	17
18	19	20	21	22	23	24
25	26	27	28	29	30	31

AUGUST • 2021

S	M	T	W	T	F	S
1	2	3	4	5	6	7
8	9	10	11	12	13	14
15	16	17	18	19	20	21
22	23	24	25	26	27	28
29	30	31				

Friday 23

FULL BUCK MOON

Saturday 24

National Day of the Cowboy

Pioneer Day (Utah)

*If you're ridin' ahead
of the herd, take a
look back every now
and then to make sure
that it's still there.*

–traditional cowboy saying

Sunday 25

HIC, HIC, HOORAY!
To cure hiccups,
use your tongue to
rub a teaspoonful of
sugar against the
roof of your mouth,
toward the back.

JULY

REMINDERS

....
....
....
....
....
....

July August

26 *Monday*

According to experts, tomatoes taste best 5 days after harvest.

27 *Tuesday*

On this day in 1943, Col. Joseph Duckworth became the first pilot to deliberately fly through a hurricane. Some call him "the father of instrument flying."

28 *Wednesday*

A day without sunshine is like, you know, night.

–Steve Martin, American comedian (b. 1945)

29 *Thursday*

Palindrome (something that reads the same forward or backward) for a summer day: "too hot to hoot."

JULY • 2021							AUGUST • 2021						
S	M	T	W	T	F	S	S	M	T	W	T	F	S
				1	2	3	1	2	3	4	5	6	7
4	5	6	7	8	9	10	8	9	10	11	12	13	14
11	12	13	14	15	16	17	15	16	17	18	19	20	21
18	19	20	21	22	23	24	22	23	24	25	26	27	28
25	26	27	28	29	30	31	29	30	31				

Friday **30**

On this day in 1956,
President Dwight D.
Eisenhower signed a
law declaring "In God
We Trust" to be the
nation's official motto.

Saturday **31**

LAST QUARTER

Sunday **1**

Colorado Day

The tallest mountain in
Colorado is Mt. Elbert,
at 14,440 feet.

REMINDERS

....
....
....
....
....
....

125 Years Ago

August 1896

Look over the fences around the pastures, and mend the weak places before the cattle break through and find their way into the cornfield of your neighbor.

—The Old Farmer's Almanac

**AUGUST 22
FULL STURGEON MOON**

A fog in August
indicates a severe
winter and plenty
of snow.

*A dreamy day; and tranquilly I lie
At anchor from all storms of mental strain;
With absent vision, gazing at the sky,
"Like one that hears it rain."*

–"A Summer Afternoon," by James Whitcomb Riley, American poet (1849–1916)

–Pixabay

12 Facts About the Number 21

In badminton, 21 points often wins a game. It is also the highest possible winning score in blackjack.

THE MONTH OF AUGUST

SUNDAY	MONDAY	TUESDAY	WEDNESDAY	THURSDAY	FRIDAY	SATURDAY
1	2	3	4	5	6	7
8	9	10	11	12	13	14
15	16	17	18	19	20	21
22	23	24	25	26	27	28
29	30	31				

For this month's holidays and Moon phases, see the weekly calendar pages that follow.

August

2 Monday

Civic Holiday (Canada)

Our hopes are high. Our faith in the people is great. Our courage is strong. And our dreams for this beautiful country will never die.

–Pierre Elliott Trudeau, 15th prime minister of Canada (1919–2000)

3 Tuesday

The average American home contains some 300,000 items.

4 Wednesday

One never loseth by doing good turns.

5 Thursday

The side of a hammer's head is called the cheek.

AUGUST • 2021							SEPTEMBER • 2021						
S	M	T	W	T	F	S	S	M	T	W	T	F	S
1	2	3	4	5	6	7				1	2	3	4
8	9	10	11	12	13	14	5	6	7	8	9	10	11
15	16	17	18	19	20	21	12	13	14	15	16	17	18
22	23	24	25	26	27	28	19	20	21	22	23	24	25
29	30	31					26	27	28	29	30		

Friday 6

*What would the world
do without tea?
How did it exist?
I am glad I was not
born before tea.*

–Sydney Smith, English clergyman
(1771–1845)

Saturday 7

Folklore says that if you
bow to the new Moon
(tomorrow) and turn over
any coins in your pocket,
you will double your money
by the next new Moon.

Sunday 8

NEW MOON

First of Muharram
begins at sundown

AUGUST

REMINDERS

....
....
....
....
....
....

Get set to see everything from Moon phases to meteor showers at Almanac.com.

August

9 Monday

A colony of 15 million Mexican free-tailed bats in Bracken Cave, near San Antonio, Texas, is one of the world's largest concentrations of mammals.

10 Tuesday

Dr. Arkin
11 AM

127|
BP 74

Harvest sweet corn when silks are dark brown, husks are green, and ears are fully developed.

11 Wednesday

Dog Days end.

When a dog or cat eats grass in the morning, it will rain before nightfall.

12 Thursday

A CLOSE SHAVE French barber Jean-Jacques Perret published the first book on shaving *(La Pogonotomie)* in 1769.

AUGUST • 2021

S	M	T	W	T	F	S
1	2	3	4	5	6	7
8	9	10	11	12	13	14
15	16	17	18	19	20	21
22	23	24	25	26	27	28
29	30	31				

SEPTEMBER • 2021

S	M	T	W	T	F	S
			1	2	3	4
5	6	7	8	9	10	11
12	13	14	15	16	17	18
19	20	21	22	23	24	25
26	27	28	29	30		

Friday 13

Months that have a
Friday the 13th always
begin on Sunday.

Saturday 14

Q. What has
to be broken before
it is used?
A. An egg.

Sunday 15

FIRST QUARTER

AUGUST

REMINDERS

....

....

....

....

....

....

Get set to see everything from Moon phases to meteor showers at Almanac.com.

August

16 Monday

Bennington Battle Day (Vt.)
Discovery Day (Y.T.)

The name "Yukon"
comes from the
Loucheux word
yu-kun-ah, meaning
"great river."

17 Tuesday

Zeal is like fire:
It wants both feeding
and watching.

18 Wednesday

SPOONERISMS
"Three cheers for
our queer old dean!"
unscrambled is
"Three cheers for our
dear old Queen!"

19 Thursday

National Aviation Day

*Let us hope that the
advent of a successful
flying machine will . . .
hasten the promised
era in which there
shall be nothing but
peace and goodwill
among all men.*

–Octave Chanute, *Progress in
Flying Machines*, 1894

AUGUST • 2021

S	M	T	W	T	F	S
1	2	3	4	5	6	7
8	9	10	11	12	13	14
15	16	17	18	19	20	21
22	23	24	25	26	27	28
29	30	31				

SEPTEMBER • 2021

S	M	T	W	T	F	S
			1	2	3	4
5	6	7	8	9	10	11
12	13	14	15	16	17	18
19	20	21	22	23	24	25
26	27	28	29	30		

Friday 20

According to U.S. Customs, an antique is an item that is at least 100 years old.

Saturday 21

About 21 percent of registered commercial drones are used in agriculture.

Sunday 22

FULL STURGEON MOON

AUGUST

REMINDERS

....
....
....
....
....
....

Get set to see everything from Moon phases to meteor showers at Almanac.com.

August

23 *Monday*

Averaging 6 feet
in length, the
South African
giant earthworm
(Microchaetus rappi)
can grow to be
as long as 22 feet.

24 *Tuesday*

*Minds are like
parachutes: They only
function when open.*
–Thomas Robert Dewar, Scottish
distiller (1864–1930)

25 *Wednesday*

HIC, HIC, HOORAY!
According to folklore,
laying a broom on
the floor and jumping
over it six times
will cure hiccups.

26 *Thursday*

BP
123/74

Dr. Panik
10 AM

Women's Equality Day

*The practice of putting
women on pedestals
began to die out when
it was discovered that
they could give orders
better from there.*
–Betty Grable, American actress
(1916–73)

AUGUST • 2021

S	M	T	W	T	F	S
1	2	3	4	5	6	7
8	9	10	11	12	13	14
15	16	17	18	19	20	21
22	23	24	25	26	27	28
29	30	31				

SEPTEMBER • 2021

S	M	T	W	T	F	S
			1	2	3	4
5	6	7	8	9	10	11
12	13	14	15	16	17	18
19	20	21	22	23	24	25
26	27	28	29	30		

Friday 27

Pickling cucumbers tend to have thinner, less bitter skins than slicing types. This allows the pickling solution to better penetrate the surface.

Saturday 28

When eager bites
the thirsty flea,
Clouds and rain you
sure shall see.

Sunday 29

On this day in 2005, Hurricane Katrina struck New Orleans and the Mississippi Gulf Coast.

AUGUST

REMINDERS

....
....
....
....
....
....

Get set to see everything from Moon phases to meteor showers at Almanac.com.

August ✿ September

30 Monday

LAST QUARTER

31 Tuesday

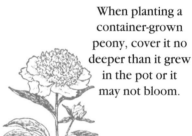

When planting a
container-grown
peony, cover it no
deeper than it grew
in the pot or it
may not bloom.

1 Wednesday

*The 2022 Old Farmer's
Almanac* is available now

2 Thursday

Dr. Paulk
Teleconference
2:20 PM

A CLOSE SHAVE
English fashion icon
Beau Brummel
(1778–1840) shaved
several times a day.

AUGUST • 2021	SEPTEMBER • 2021
S M T W T F S	S M T W T F S
1 2 3 4 5 6 7	1 2 3 4
8 9 10 11 12 13 14	5 6 7 8 9 10 11
15 16 17 18 19 20 21	12 13 14 15 16 17 18
22 23 24 25 26 27 28	19 20 21 22 23 24 25
29 30 31	26 27 28 29 30

Friday 3

On this day in 1929, the Dow Jones industrial average closed at 381.17, its peak before the crash of October that led to the Great Depression.

Saturday 4

If you can't fall asleep, try yawning. Keep on yawning until you feel sleepy.

Sunday 5

Store winter squashes and pumpkins under a bed in an unheated room.

AUG/SEP

REMINDERS

....
....
....
....
....
....

Get set to see everything from Moon phases to meteor showers at Almanac.com.

125 Years Ago

September 1896

Give your sons who are to become farmers an education adapted to their chosen occupation. There are plenty of agricultural schools where they can take a one-, two-, or four-year course; any of these will be of great benefit to them.

–*The Old Farmer's Almanac*

**SEPTEMBER 20
FULL HARVEST MOON**

If St. Michael (Sept. 29) brings many acorns, Christmas will cover the fields with snow.

Of all the seasons, autumn offers the most to man and requires the least of him.

–Hal Borland, American naturalist (1900–78)

The NEW YORK Sun

TUESDAY, SEPTEMBER 21, 1897

Is there a Santa Claus?

We take pleasure in answering at once and thus prominently the communication below, expressing at the same time our great gratification that its faithful author is numbered among the friends of THE SUN:

Dear Editor: I am 8 years old.
Some of my little friends say there is no Santa Claus.
Papa says, "If you see it in THE SUN it's so."
Please tell me the truth, is there a Santa Claus?

**Virginia O'Hanlon
115 West-Ninety-Fifth Street**

Virginia, your little friends are wrong. They have been affected by the skepticism of a skeptical age. They do not believe except what they see. They think that nothing can be which is not comprehensible by their little minds. All minds, Virginia, whether they be men's or children's, are little. In this great universe of ours, man is a mere insect, an ant, in his intellect as compared with the boundless world about him, as measured by the intelligence capable of grasping the whole of truth and knowledge.

Yes, Virginia, there is a Santa Claus. He exists as certainly as love and generosity and devotion exist, and you know that they abound and give to your life its highest beauty and joy. Alas! How dreary would be the world if there were no Santa Claus. It would be as dreary as if there were no Virginias.

There would be no childlike faith then, no poetry, no romance to make tolerable this existence. We should have no enjoyment, except in sense and sight. The external light with which childhood fills the world would be extinguished.

Not believe in Santa Claus! You might as well not believe in fairies. You might get your papa to hire men to watch in all the chimneys on Christmas Eve to catch Santa Claus, but even if you did not see Santa Claus coming down, what would that prove? Nobody sees Santa Claus, but that is no sign that there is no Santa Claus. The most real things in the world are those that neither children nor men can see. Did you ever see fairies dancing on the lawn? Of course not, but that's no proof that they are not there. Nobody can conceive or imagine all the wonders there are unseen and unseeable in the world.

You tear apart the baby's rattle and see what makes the noise inside, but there is a veil covering the unseen world which not the strongest man, nor even the united strength of all the strongest men that ever lived could tear apart. Only faith, poetry, love, romance, can push aside that curtain and view and picture the supernal beauty and glory beyond. Is it all real? Ah, Virginia, in all this world there is nothing else real and abiding. No Santa Claus! Thank God! He lives and lives forever. A thousand years from now, Virginia, nay 10 times 10,000 years from now, he will continue to make glad the heart of childhood.

12 Facts About the Number 21

On September 21, 1897, in response to a question from 8-year-old Virginia O'Hanlon, *The New York Sun* printed an anonymous editorial that replied, "Yes, Virginia, there is a Santa Claus." Written by Francis Church, it is believed to be the most frequently reprinted newspaper editorial in history.

THE MONTH OF SEPTEMBER

SUNDAY	MONDAY	TUESDAY	WEDNESDAY	THURSDAY	FRIDAY	SATURDAY
			1	2	3	4
5	6	7	8	9	10	11
12	13	14	15	16	17	18
19	20	21	22	23	24	25
26	27	28	29	30		

For this month's holidays and Moon phases, see the weekly calendar pages that follow.

September

6 *Monday*

NEW MOON

Rosh Hashanah
begins at sundown
Labor Day

7 *Tuesday*

When a camel is at
the foot of a mountain, then
judge of his height.

8 *Wednesday*

On a clear and
moonless night away
from bright lights,
you can see about
2,500 stars.

9 *Thursday*

Admission Day (Calif.)

On this day in which
year did California
become a state?

a. 1846

b. 1848

c. 1850

Answer: c

SEPTEMBER • 2021	OCTOBER • 2021
S M T W T F S	S M T W T F S
1 2 3 4	1 2
5 6 7 8 9 10 11	3 4 5 6 7 8 9
12 13 14 15 16 17 18	10 11 12 13 14 15 16
19 20 21 22 23 24 25	17 18 19 20 21 22 23
26 27 28 29 30	24 25 26 27 28 29 30
	31

Friday **10**

Seed new lawns before
the leaves fall.

Saturday **11**

Patriot Day

Two bars or bugles
on a uniform can
indicate the rank
of captain in a
firefighting company.

Sunday **12**

Grandparents Day

*A grandfather is
someone with
silver in his hair and
gold in his heart.*
—unknown

SEPTEMBER

REMINDERS

....
....
....
....
....

Got apples? Bake a treat from Almanac.com.

September

13 *Monday*

FIRST QUARTER

14 *Tuesday*

About 6 percent of
Americans are vegans.

15 *Wednesday*

Yom Kippur begins
at sundown

*The only man who
never makes a
mistake is the man
who never does
anything.*

–Theodore Roosevelt, 26th U.S.
president (1858–1919)

16 *Thursday*

To float in water,
armadillos gulp air to
inflate their stomachs
and intestines.

SEPTEMBER • 2021							OCTOBER • 2021						
S	M	T	W	T	F	S	S	M	T	W	T	F	S
			1	2	3	4						1	2
5	6	7	8	9	10	11	3	4	5	6	7	8	9
12	13	14	15	16	17	18	10	11	12	13	14	15	16
19	20	21	22	23	24	25	17	18	19	20	21	22	23
26	27	28	29	30			24	25	26	27	28	29	30
							31						

Friday 17

Constitution Day

In 1787, the U.S. Constitution was written in secret behind closed doors in the Pennsylvania State House in Philadelphia. Sentries were on guard.

Saturday 18

SPOONERISMS
"Please sew me to another sheet" unscrambled is "Please show me to another seat."

Sunday 19

Clear and dry and providential, Then potentially torrential!
–The Old Farmer's Almanac, 2006

SEPTEMBER

REMINDERS

....

....

....

....

....

....

Got apples? Bake a treat from Almanac.com.

September

20 *Monday*

FULL HARVEST MOON

21 *Tuesday*

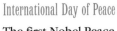

22 *Wednesday*

Autumnal Equinox

As the wind and
weather at the equinoxes,
so will they be for
the next 3 months.

23 *Thursday*

On this day in 1806,
the Lewis and Clark
expedition arrived back
in St. Louis, Missouri.

SEPTEMBER • 2021

S	M	T	W	T	F	S
			1	2	3	4
5	6	7	8	9	10	11
12	13	14	15	16	17	18
19	20	21	22	23	24	25
26	27	28	29	30		

OCTOBER • 2021

S	M	T	W	T	F	S
					1	2
3	4	5	6	7	8	9
10	11	12	13	14	15	16
17	18	19	20	21	22	23
24	25	26	27	28	29	30
31						

Friday 24

Brussels sprouts and parsnips taste sweeter after they've been exposed to frost.

Saturday 25

HIC, HIC, HOORAY! To cure hiccups, breathe slowly into a paper bag for a few minutes (discontinue if you feel dizzy).

Sunday 26

On this day in 1960, the first televised presidential debate, between candidates Richard M. Nixon and John F. Kennedy, took place.

SEPTEMBER

REMINDERS

....

....

....

....

....

....

Got apples? Bake a treat from Almanac.com.

September ❦ October

27 *Monday*

Roughly 80 percent of American collectors wish to leave their collections to heirs, but only about 35 percent of the inheritors really want them.

28 *Tuesday*

LAST QUARTER

29 *Wednesday*

I've got to follow them; I am their leader.

–Alexandre Auguste Ledru-Rollin, French politician (1807–74)

30 *Thursday*

According to some studies, students exposed to the color red before taking an exam scored lower than those exposed to black, gray, green, or white.

SEPTEMBER • 2021	OCTOBER • 2021
S M T W T F S	S M T W T F S
1 2 3 4	1 2
5 6 7 8 9 10 11	3 4 5 6 7 8 9
12 13 14 15 16 17 18	10 11 12 13 14 15 16
19 20 21 22 23 24 25	17 18 19 20 21 22 23
26 27 28 29 30	24 25 26 27 28 29 30
	31

Friday

1

Ideas should be clear
and chocolate thick.
–Spanish proverb

Saturday

2

In Oregon's Malheur
National Forest,
an underground
mushroom spans some
2,385 acres. It is the
world's largest and
perhaps longest-known
organism.

Sunday

3

When making piecrust,
cut ventilation holes
into creative shapes:
stars, hearts, or leaves.

SEP/OCT

REMINDERS

....

....

....

....

....

....

Got apples? Bake a treat from Almanac.com.

125 Years Ago

October 1896

When a man gets the idea into his head that he knows how to do everything better than anyone else, it is about time for him to compare notes with others and be examined by an impartial committee.

–The Old Farmer's Almanac

**OCTOBER 20
FULL HUNTER'S MOON**

**Warm October,
cold February.**

October: This is one of the peculiarly dangerous months to speculate in stocks. The others are July, January, September, April, November, May, March, June, December, August, and February.

–Mark Twain, American writer (1835–1910)

–The Accolade, by Edmund Blair Leighton

12 Facts About the Number 21

In medieval England, a squire usually became a knight at 21, after proving his loyalty and service.

THE MONTH OF OCTOBER

SUNDAY	MONDAY	TUESDAY	WEDNESDAY	THURSDAY	FRIDAY	SATURDAY
					1	2
3	4	5	6	7	8	9
10	11	12	13	14	15	16
17	18	19	20	21	22	23
24 / 31	25	26	27	28	29	30

For this month's holidays and Moon phases, see the weekly calendar pages that follow.

October

4 Monday

5 Tuesday

On this day in
1925, WSM radio in
Nashville, Tennessee,
debuted. On
November 28, the
station produced the
first broadcast of
the "Grand Ole Opry,"
on its *WSM Barn
Dance* program.

6 Wednesday

NEW MOON

7 Thursday

Ease a headache
by drinking tomato
juice blended
with fresh basil.

OCTOBER • 2021

S	M	T	W	T	F	S
					1	2
3	4	5	6	7	8	9
10	11	12	13	14	15	16
17	18	19	20	21	22	23
24	25	26	27	28	29	30
31						

NOVEMBER • 2021

S	M	T	W	T	F	S
	1	2	3	4	5	6
7	8	9	10	11	12	13
14	15	16	17	18	19	20
21	22	23	24	25	26	27
28	29	30				

Friday 8

Grasp no more than thy
hand will hold.

Saturday 9

Leif Eriksson Day

*Adventure is allowing
the unexpected to
happen to you.*
–Richard Aldington, English
writer (1892–1962)

Sunday 10

On this day in 1971,
the reconstructed
London Bridge
reopened in Lake
Havasu City, Arizona,
after having been
shipped all the way
from England.

REMINDERS

....
....
....
....
....
....

OCTOBER

Will the weather trick or treat? Find out at Almanac.com.

October

11 Monday

Columbus Day, observed
Indigenous Peoples' Day
Thanksgiving Day (Canada)

*Gratitude is not
only the greatest of
virtues, but the parent
of all others.*
–Cicero, Roman statesman
(106 B.C.–43 B.C.)

12 Tuesday

FIRST QUARTER

13 Wednesday

A CLOSE SHAVE
In 1847, William
Henson invented the
"hoe razor," which was
the first to have the
blade perpendicular
to the handle.

14 Thursday

To preserve flavor
and prevent pitted
or stained cookware,
avoid using aluminum
pans when cooking
with tomatoes.

OCTOBER • 2021							NOVEMBER • 2021					
S	M	T	W	T	F	S	S	M	T	W	T	F	S
					1	2		1	2	3	4	5	6
3	4	5	6	7	8	9	7	8	9	10	11	12	13
10	11	12	13	14	15	16	14	15	16	17	18	19	20
17	18	19	20	21	22	23	21	22	23	24	25	26	27
24	25	26	27	28	29	30	28	29	30				
31												

Friday 15

On this day in 1984,
3 feet of snow fell
near Colorado Springs,
one of the earliest
snowstorms ever to
occur in this region.

Saturday 16

Preserve fall leaves
by boiling one part
glycerin with two parts
water. Soak leaves
and stems in the
solution overnight.

Sunday 17

Be not a baker if your
head be of butter.
–Spanish proverb

REMINDERS

....
....
....
....
....

Will the weather trick or treat? Find out at Almanac.com.

OCTOBER

October

18 *Monday*

Alaska Day

Alaska is the only state name that you can type by using just one row of a standard U.S. keyboard.

19 *Tuesday*

A 6-year-old once said: "For centuries, people thought the Moon was made of green cheese. Then the astronauts found that the Moon is really a big hard rock. That's what happens to cheese when you leave it out."

20 *Wednesday*

FULL HUNTER'S MOON

21 *Thursday*

SPOONERISMS
"Is the bean dizzy?"
unscrambled is
"Is the dean busy?"

OCTOBER • 2021   NOVEMBER • 2021

S	M	T	W	T	F	S		S	M	T	W	T	F	S
					1	2			1	2	3	4	5	6
3	4	5	6	7	8	9		7	8	9	10	11	12	13
10	11	12	13	14	15	16		14	15	16	17	18	19	20
17	18	19	20	21	22	23		21	22	23	24	25	26	27
24	25	26	27	28	29	30		28	29	30				
31														

Friday **22**

If you dream of rubber,
it means that you are
adaptable and versatile.

Saturday **23**

While planting bulbs,
add a handful
of pea gravel on top
of each to
discourage voles.

Sunday **24**

United Nations Day

United Nations Day
has been celebrated on
October 24 in every
year since 1948.

OCTOBER

REMINDERS

....
....
....
....
....
....

Will the weather trick or treat? Find out at Almanac.com.

October

25 *Monday*

HIC, HIC, HOORAY!
To cure hiccups,
swallow 1 teaspoon
of vinegar.

26 *Tuesday*

For fatter spears
next year, top
asparagus plants
with aged compost
or manure now.

27 *Wednesday*

*Nothing will stop
you being creative
more effectively
than the fear of
making a mistake.*
–John Cleese, English comedian,
born on this day in 1939

28 *Thursday*

LAST QUARTER

OCTOBER • 2021	NOVEMBER • 2021
S M T W T F S	S M T W T F S
1 2	1 2 3 4 5 6
3 4 5 6 7 8 9	7 8 9 10 11 12 13
10 11 12 13 14 15 16	14 15 16 17 18 19 20
17 18 19 20 21 22 23	21 22 23 24 25 26 27
24 25 26 27 28 29 30	28 29 30
31	

Nevada Day
Friday 29

More than 100,000
couples get married
in Las Vegas, Nevada,
every year.

Saturday 30

Ancient Egyptians
used thyme
oil for embalming.

Halloween
Sunday 31

Folklore advises you to
bury a dime under your hog
pen to keep witches away.

REMINDERS

....

....

....

....

....

....

OCTOBER

Will the weather trick or treat? Find out at Almanac.com.

125 Years Ago

November 1896

November is one of the best months in the year to cut wood. The weather is cool, the ground is usually clear of snow, and the quality of the wood is much better than if cut later in the season.

–The Old Farmer's Almanac

NOVEMBER 19
FULL BEAVER MOON

November take flail,
let ships no more sail.

Implacable November weather. As much mud in the streets as if the waters had but newly retired from the face of the earth, and it would not be wonderful to meet a Megalosaurus, forty feet long or so, waddling like an elephantine lizard up Holborn Hill.

–Bleak House, by Charles Dickens, English writer (1812–70)

–XL Recordings

12 Facts About the Number 21

Pop singer Adele's second studio album, *21,* was named after her age at the time she recorded it. When it was released, *Billboard* magazine called it the greatest record album of all time.

The Month of November

SUNDAY	MONDAY	TUESDAY	WEDNESDAY	THURSDAY	FRIDAY	SATURDAY
	1	2	3	4	5	6
7	8	9	10	11	12	13
14	15	16	17	18	19	20
21	22	23	24	25	26	27
28	29	30				

For this month's holidays and Moon phases, see the weekly calendar pages that follow.

November

1 Monday

If All Saints' (today) brings out winter, St. Martin's (Nov. 11) brings out Indian Summer.

2 Tuesday

Election Day

Politics has become so expensive that it takes a lot of money even to be defeated.
–Will Rogers, American humorist (1879–1935)

3 Wednesday

Oklahoma's state vegetable is the watermelon.

4 Thursday

NEW MOON

Will Rogers Day (Okla.)

NOVEMBER • 2021	DECEMBER • 2021
S M T W T F S	S M T W T F S
1 2 3 4 5 6	1 2 3 4
7 8 9 10 11 12 13	5 6 7 8 9 10 11
14 15 16 17 18 19 20	12 13 14 15 16 17 18
21 22 23 24 25 26 27	19 20 21 22 23 24 25
28 29 30	26 27 28 29 30 31

Friday 5

December gets busy:
Make appointments
for haircuts now.

Saturday 6

On this day in 2005, a
powerful F3 tornado
struck areas of
Kentucky and Indiana,
including Evansville,
taking the lives of
25 people. It was one
of the deadliest single
tornadoes on record.

Sunday 7

Daylight Saving Time
ends at 2:00 A.M.

Time devours all things.

REMINDERS

....

....

....

....

....

NOVEMBER

November

8 *Monday*

To make butternut squash easier to cut and peel, pierce the skin in a few places and then microwave the squash for 2 to 3 minutes.

9 *Tuesday*

It is not always granted to the sower to see the harvest.

–Albert Schweitzer, French philosopher and missionary physician (1875–1965)

10 *Wednesday*

U.S. Marine Corps Birthday

When U.S. Marines celebrate this day, the first three pieces of birthday cake are presented to the guest of honor and the oldest and youngest Marines present.

11 *Thursday*

FIRST QUARTER

Veterans Day
Remembrance Day (Canada)

NOVEMBER • 2021							DECEMBER • 2021						
S	M	T	W	T	F	S	S	M	T	W	T	F	S
	1	2	3	4	5	6				1	2	3	4
7	8	9	10	11	12	13	5	6	7	8	9	10	11
14	15	16	17	18	19	20	12	13	14	15	16	17	18
21	22	23	24	25	26	27	19	20	21	22	23	24	25
28	29	30					26	27	28	29	30	31	

Friday **12**

A CLOSE SHAVE
American entrepreneur
King Gillette invented
disposable razor
blades in 1895.

Saturday **13**

Where doubt is, truth is.

Sunday **14**

A white speck on the nail
of your little finger foretells
a new sweetheart.

REMINDERS

....
....
....
....
....

Thanks for using this calendar—and for visiting Almanac.com!

November

15 Monday

On this day in 1805, the Lewis and Clark expedition reached the Pacific Ocean.

16 Tuesday

Indecision may or may not be my problem.

–Jimmy Buffett, American musician (b. 1946)

17 Wednesday

When you are asleep, the discs that separate the vertebrae in the spinal column expand slightly, making you a little taller; during the day, they compress again.

18 Thursday

SPOONERISMS
"A nosy little cook" unscrambled is "a cozy little nook."

NOVEMBER • 2021	DECEMBER • 2021
S M T W T F S	S M T W T F S
1 2 3 4 5 6	1 2 3 4
7 8 9 10 11 12 13	5 6 7 8 9 10 11
14 15 16 17 18 19 20	12 13 14 15 16 17 18
21 22 23 24 25 26 27	19 20 21 22 23 24 25
28 29 30	26 27 28 29 30 31

Friday 19

FULL BEAVER MOON

Discovery of
Puerto Rico Day

Partial Lunar Eclipse
(visible in parts of N.Am.)

Saturday 20

National Child Day (Canada)

Mix together black
oil sunflower seeds,
safflower seeds, and
chopped, unsalted
peanuts for the birds.

Sunday 21

HIC, HIC, HOORAY!
To cure hiccups,
pull up your knees to
your chest.

R EMINDERS

....
....
....
....
....
....

NOVEMBER

November

22 Monday

Cheerfulness keeps up a kind of daylight in the mind and fills it with a steady and perpetual serenity.

–Joseph Addison,
English writer (1672–1719)

23 Tuesday

To avoid tears, put onions in the freezer for a few minutes before slicing.

24 Wednesday

According to folklore, if you suspect that your turkeys are bewitched, throw a handful of salt onto your fire.

25 Thursday

Thanksgiving Day

Contrary to popular belief, Pilgrim men did not wear buckles on their hats or shoes.

NOVEMBER • 2021							DECEMBER • 2021						
S	M	T	W	T	F	S	S	M	T	W	T	F	S
	1	2	3	4	5	6				1	2	3	4
7	8	9	10	11	12	13	5	6	7	8	9	10	11
14	15	16	17	18	19	20	12	13	14	15	16	17	18
21	22	23	24	25	26	27	19	20	21	22	23	24	25
28	29	30					26	27	28	29	30	31	

Friday 26

Acadian Day (La.)

Acadians are descendants of the French-speaking inhabitants of Acadia (Canada) who were expelled from the region by the British in 1755.

Saturday 27

LAST QUARTER

Sunday 28

Chanukah begins at sundown

During Chanukah, the shammash candle is used to light the others on a menorah. It rests on a branch set either higher or lower than the other eight.

R E M I N D E R S

....
....
....
....
....
....

NOVEMBER

Thanks for using this calendar—and for visiting Almanac.com!

November ✣ December

29 *Monday*

Always enter a new home with a loaf of bread and a new broom.

30 *Tuesday*

Archaeologists in Peru discovered avocado seeds buried with Incan mummies that date from 750 B.C.

1 *Wednesday*

To remove a scratch on wood furniture, rub a shelled walnut over it. Smooth the area with your fingers, wait several minutes, and then buff with a soft cloth.

2 *Thursday*

Who looks not before, finds himself behind.

NOVEMBER • 2021

S	M	T	W	T	F	S
	1	2	3	4	5	6
7	8	9	10	11	12	13
14	15	16	17	18	19	20
21	22	23	24	25	26	27
28	29	30				

DECEMBER • 2021

S	M	T	W	T	F	S
			1	2	3	4
5	6	7	8	9	10	11
12	13	14	15	16	17	18
19	20	21	22	23	24	25
26	27	28	29	30	31	

Friday

3

In about 600 million years, there will be no more total solar eclipses. The lunar orbit will have expanded to the point where the Moon will appear too small to completely cover the Sun.

Saturday

4

NEW MOON

Total Solar Eclipse
(not visible in N.Am.)

Sunday

5

*Quote me as saying
I was misquoted.*

–Groucho Marx, American
comedian (1890–1977)

REMINDERS

....
....
....
....
....
....

Thanks for using this calendar—and for visiting Almanac.com!

125 Years Ago

December 1896

A few hours of reading useful books each day during the winter will make wonderful progress in educating a man; and when he once gets into the habit of reading for improvement, he finds it a great pleasure.

–The Old Farmer's Almanac

DECEMBER 18
FULL COLD MOON

Snow on Christmas
night, good
hop crop next year.

I wonder if the snow loves the trees and fields, that it kisses them so gently?

–Alice in *Through the Looking-Glass*, by Lewis Carroll, English writer (1832–98)

–Fernando Frazão/Agência Brasil

12 Facts About the Number 21

People born on the 21st day of a month include: Revolutionary War hero Ethan Allen (Jan. 1738), poet W. H. Auden (Feb. 1907), actor Gary Oldman (Mar. 1958), Queen Elizabeth II (Apr. 1926), King Philip II of Spain (May 1527), philosopher Jean-Paul Sartre (June 1905), novelist Ernest Hemingway (July 1899), sprinter Usain Bolt (Aug. 1986), writer Stephen King (Sept. 1947), actress Carrie Fisher (Oct. 1956), singer Björk (Nov. 1965), and tennis player Chris Evert (Dec. 1954).

THE MONTH OF DECEMBER

SUNDAY	MONDAY	TUESDAY	WEDNESDAY	THURSDAY	FRIDAY	SATURDAY
			1	2	3	4
5	6	7	8	9	10	11
12	13	14	15	16	17	18
19	20	21	22	23	24	25
26	27	28	29	30	31	

For this month's holidays and Moon phases, see the weekly calendar pages that follow.

December

6 Monday

If you dream of a hedgehog, it may mean that you have a prickly choice to make that might cost you a friend.

7 Tuesday

National Pearl Harbor Remembrance Day

Pearl Harbor in Oahu, Hawaii, once housed many pearl oysters, hence its original Hawaiian name of Wai Momi ("pearl waters").

8 Wednesday

A proverb is the wit of one and the wisdom of many.
–Lord John Russell, British prime minister (1792–1878)

9 Thursday

Q: What do you call a camel without a hump?

A: Humphrey

DECEMBER • 2021

S	M	T	W	T	F	S
			1	2	3	4
5	6	7	8	9	10	11
12	13	14	15	16	17	18
19	20	21	22	23	24	25
26	27	28	29	30	31	

JANUARY • 2022

S	M	T	W	T	F	S
						1
2	3	4	5	6	7	8
9	10	11	12	13	14	15
16	17	18	19	20	21	22
23	24	25	26	27	28	29
30	31					

Friday 10

FIRST QUARTER

Saturday 11

About 300 million years ago, there were not seven continents on Earth, but one supercontinent, Pangaea.

Sunday 12

A CLOSE SHAVE
Jacob Schick patented the first successful electric razor in 1928.

REMINDERS

....
....
....
....
....
....

December

13 *Monday*

14 *Tuesday*

Halcyon Days, 2 weeks
of calm weather near
the winter solstice,
comes from an ancient
Greek belief that
the kingfisher, or
"halcyon," quieted the
wind and waves while
hatching its eggs on
a nest in the sea.

15 *Wednesday*

Bill of Rights Day

*Government is the
creature of the people.*
−Rev. Robert Hall, English
minister (1764–1831)

16 *Thursday*

Cream of tartar is
a salt left behind
when grapes ferment
into wine.

DECEMBER • 2021							JANUARY • 2022						
S	M	T	W	T	F	S	S	M	T	W	T	F	S
			1	2	3	4							1
5	6	7	8	9	10	11	2	3	4	5	6	7	8
12	13	14	15	16	17	18	9	10	11	12	13	14	15
19	20	21	22	23	24	25	16	17	18	19	20	21	22
26	27	28	29	30	31		23	24	25	26	27	28	29
							30	31					

Friday **17**

Wright Brothers Day

*Sometimes, the world
from above seems
too beautiful, too
wonderful, too distant
for human eyes to see.*

–Charles A. Lindbergh, American
aviator (1902–74)

Saturday **18**

FULL COLD MOON

Sunday **19**

Thunder during Christmas
week means much snow
during the winter.

REMINDERS

....
....
....
....
....

Need great gift ideas? Visit our shop at Almanac.com.

DECEMBER

December

20 *Monday*

SPOONERISMS
"A well-boiled icicle"
unscrambled is "a well-
oiled bicycle."

21 *Tuesday*

Winter Solstice

In many areas of the
Northern Hemisphere,
today provides the
least amount of
daylight; on this day at
the North Pole, the Sun
never rises (it hasn't
since late September).

22 *Wednesday*

A wolf's howl can
be heard from between
6 and 10 miles away.

23 *Thursday*

HIC, HIC, HOORAY!
To cure hiccups,
press your philtrum
(the groove between
nose and mouth)
for 30 seconds.

DECEMBER • 2021								JANUARY • 2022						
S	M	T	W	T	F	S		S	M	T	W	T	F	S
			1	2	3	4								1
5	6	7	8	9	10	11		2	3	4	5	6	7	8
12	13	14	15	16	17	18		9	10	11	12	13	14	15
19	20	21	22	23	24	25		16	17	18	19	20	21	22
26	27	28	29	30	31			23	24	25	26	27	28	29
								30	31					

Friday **24**

When the snow falls dry,
it means to lie;
But flakes light and soft
bring rain oft.

Saturday **25**

Christmas Day

At Christmastime
in the Philippines,
homes and streets
are decorated with
lanterns called paróls,
which are shaped like
the star of Bethlehem.

Sunday **26**

LAST QUARTER

Boxing Day (Canada)
First day of Kwanzaa

REMINDERS

....
....
....
....
....

Need great gift ideas? Visit our shop at Almanac.com.

DECEMBER

December 2021 ❧ January 2022

27 *Monday*

The 134-mile-wide
Galle Crater on Mars
has ridges that form
a smiling face.

28 *Tuesday*

Who doffs his coat on
a winter's day,
Will gladly put it on in May.

29 *Wednesday*

*You can't be brave
if you've only
had wonderful things
happen to you.*
–Mary Tyler Moore,
American actress (1936–2017)

30 *Thursday*

The northern
cardinal is the state
bird of Illinois,
Indiana, Kentucky,
North Carolina, Ohio,
Virginia, and
West Virginia.

DECEMBER • 2021

S	M	T	W	T	F	S
			1	2	3	4
5	6	7	8	9	10	11
12	13	14	15	16	17	18
19	20	21	22	23	24	25
26	27	28	29	30	31	

JANUARY • 2022

S	M	T	W	T	F	S
						1
2	3	4	5	6	7	8
9	10	11	12	13	14	15
16	17	18	19	20	21	22
23	24	25	26	27	28	29
30	31					

Friday 31

On New Year's Eve in Romania, people dress up as bears and visit other people's homes to scare away evil spirits.

Saturday 1

New Year's Day

To welcome in the newborn year, A thousand happy voices Are heard in tones of mirthful cheer, And every heart rejoices.
—*The Country Gentleman*, 1854

Sunday 2

NEW MOON

REMINDERS

Need great gift ideas? Visit our shop at Almanac.com.

DEC / JAN

2022 Advance Planner

bold = *U.S. and/or Canadian national holidays*

JANUARY • 2022

S	M	T	W	T	F	S
						1
2	3	4	5	6	7	8
9	10	11	12	13	14	15
16	**17**	18	19	20	21	22
23	24	25	26	27	28	29
30	31					

FEBRUARY • 2022

S	M	T	W	T	F	S
		1	2	3	4	5
6	7	8	9	10	11	12
13	14	15	16	17	18	19
20	**21**	22	23	24	25	26
27	28					

MARCH • 2022

S	M	T	W	T	F	S
		1	2	3	4	5
6	7	8	9	10	11	12
13	14	15	16	17	18	19
20	21	22	23	24	25	26
27	28	29	30	31		

APRIL • 2022

S	M	T	W	T	F	S
					1	2
3	4	5	6	7	8	9
10	11	12	13	14	**15**	16
17	**18**	19	20	21	22	23
24	25	26	27	28	29	30

MAY • 2022

S	M	T	W	T	F	S
1	2	3	4	5	6	7
8	9	10	11	12	13	14
15	16	17	18	19	20	21
22	**23**	24	25	26	27	28
29	**30**	31				

JUNE • 2022

S	M	T	W	T	F	S
			1	2	3	4
5	6	7	8	9	10	11
12	13	14	15	16	17	18
19	20	21	22	23	24	25
26	27	28	29	30		

JULY • 2022

S	M	T	W	T	F	S
					1	2
3	**4**	5	6	7	8	9
10	11	12	13	14	15	16
17	18	19	20	21	22	23
24	25	26	27	28	29	30
31						

AUGUST • 2022

S	M	T	W	T	F	S
	1	2	3	4	5	6
7	8	9	10	11	12	13
14	15	16	17	18	19	20
21	22	23	24	25	26	27
28	29	30	31			

SEPTEMBER • 2022

S	M	T	W	T	F	S
				1	2	3
4	**5**	6	7	8	9	10
11	12	13	14	15	16	17
18	19	20	21	22	23	24
25	26	27	28	29	30	

OCTOBER • 2022

S	M	T	W	T	F	S
						1
2	3	4	5	6	7	8
9	**10**	11	12	13	14	15
16	17	18	19	20	21	22
23	24	25	26	27	28	29
30	31					

NOVEMBER • 2022

S	M	T	W	T	F	S
		1	2	3	4	5
6	7	8	9	10	**11**	12
13	14	15	16	17	18	19
20	21	22	23	**24**	25	26
27	28	29	30			

DECEMBER • 2022

S	M	T	W	T	F	S
				1	2	3
4	5	6	7	8	9	10
11	12	13	14	15	16	17
18	19	20	21	22	23	24
25	**26**	27	28	29	30	31

2023 Advance Planner

bold = *U.S. and/or Canadian national holidays*

JANUARY • 2023

S	M	T	W	T	F	S
1	2	3	4	5	6	7
8	9	10	11	12	13	14
15	**16**	17	18	19	20	21
22	23	24	25	26	27	28
29	30	31				

FEBRUARY • 2023

S	M	T	W	T	F	S
			1	2	3	4
5	6	7	8	9	10	11
12	13	14	15	16	17	18
19	**20**	21	22	23	24	25
26	27	28				

MARCH • 2023

S	M	T	W	T	F	S
			1	2	3	4
5	6	7	8	9	10	11
12	13	14	15	16	17	18
19	20	21	22	23	24	25
26	27	28	29	30	31	

APRIL • 2023

S	M	T	W	T	F	S
						1
2	3	4	5	6	**7**	8
9	**10**	11	12	13	14	15
16	17	18	19	20	21	22
23	24	25	26	27	28	29
30						

MAY • 2023

S	M	T	W	T	F	S
	1	2	3	4	5	6
7	8	9	10	11	12	13
14	15	16	17	18	19	20
21	**22**	23	24	25	26	27
28	**29**	30	31			

JUNE • 2023

S	M	T	W	T	F	S
				1	2	3
4	5	6	7	8	9	10
11	12	13	14	15	16	17
18	19	20	21	22	23	24
25	26	27	28	29	30	

JULY • 2023

S	M	T	W	T	F	S
						1
2	3	**4**	5	6	7	8
9	10	11	12	13	14	15
16	17	18	19	20	21	22
23	24	25	26	27	28	29
30	31					

AUGUST • 2023

S	M	T	W	T	F	S
		1	2	3	4	5
6	7	8	9	10	11	12
13	14	15	16	17	18	19
20	21	22	23	24	25	26
27	28	29	30	31		

SEPTEMBER • 2023

S	M	T	W	T	F	S
					1	2
3	**4**	5	6	7	8	9
10	11	12	13	14	15	16
17	18	19	20	21	22	23
24	25	26	27	28	29	30

OCTOBER • 2023

S	M	T	W	T	F	S
1	2	3	4	5	6	7
8	**9**	10	11	12	13	14
15	16	17	18	19	20	21
22	23	24	25	26	27	28
29	30	31				

NOVEMBER • 2023

S	M	T	W	T	F	S
			1	2	3	4
5	6	7	8	9	10	**11**
12	13	14	15	16	17	18
19	20	21	22	**23**	24	25
26	27	28	29	30		

DECEMBER • 2023

S	M	T	W	T	F	S
					1	2
3	4	5	6	7	8	9
10	11	12	13	14	15	16
17	18	19	20	21	22	23
24	**25**	**26**	27	28	29	30
31						

Planning a trip? See the Long-Range Weather Forecast at Almanac.com/Weather.

Passwords

Web site	User name	Password

Addresses and Phone Numbers

Name _____ Home _____

Address _____ Work _____

_____ Cell _____

Email _____ Fax _____

Web site _____

Name _____ Home _____

Address _____ Work _____

_____ Cell _____

Email _____ Fax _____

Web site _____

Name _____ Home _____

Address _____ Work _____

_____ Cell _____

Email _____ Fax _____

Web site _____

Name _____ Home _____

Address _____ Work _____

_____ Cell _____

Email _____ Fax _____

Web site _____

Name _____ Home _____

Address _____ Work _____

_____ Cell _____

Email _____ Fax _____

Web site _____

Name _____ Home _____

Address _____ Work _____

_____ Cell _____

Email _____ Fax _____

Web site _____

Emergency Contacts

In case of emergency, notify:

Name   Relationship

Address

Phone (Home)   (Work)   (Cell)

Email

Police department

Fire department

Ambulance

Hospital

Poison control

Physician

Dentist

Veterinarian

Pharmacy

Clergy

Phone company

Internet provider

Electric company

Electrician

Plumber

Auto mechanic

Baby-sitter

School(s)

Insurance:

   Auto

   Homeowner's

   Health

   Dental

Other